Robert Quackenbush

ONCE UPON A TIME!
A Story of the Brothers Grimm

Simon and Schuster Books for Young Readers
Published by Simon & Schuster Inc., New York

Simon and Schuster Books for Young Readers

Simon & Schuster Building
Rockefeller Center
1230 Avenue of the Americas
New York, New York 10020

10 9 8 7 6 5 4 3

Library of Congress Cat. in Pub. Data—tk

Quackenbush, Robert M.
   Once upon a time!

   Summary: Recounts the lives of two German brothers
who collected folktales such as "Hansel and Gretel"
and "Rumpelstiltskin" in order to preserve them for future generations.
   1. Grimm, Jacob, 1785-1863—Juvenile literature.
2. Grimm, Wilhelm, 1780-1859—Juvenile literature.
3. Philologists—Germany—Biography—Juvenile
literature. [1. Grimm, Jacob, 1785-1863. 2. Grimm,
Wilhelm, 1786-1859. 3. Philologists] I. Title.
PD63.Q3   1985   398.2′1′0922[B]   [920]   85-9410
ISBN 0-671-66296-1

Once upon a time (this is a true story), there were two brothers named Jacob and Wilhelm Grimm. Jacob was born on January 4, 1785. Wilhelm was born on February 24, 1786. They were the oldest of six children. Being so close in age—just over one year apart—they were like twins. They did everything together. They got up at the same time in the morning, they ate the same breakfast, they read the same books, and they went to bed at the same time every night. They especially liked taking long walks in the country together to collect things like butterflies and birds' eggs. They would trade some of the things they found for things they liked more—like colored stones from their friends' collections. They were born barterers.

9

Jacob and Wilhelm lived in a house surrounded by cows, chickens, horses, sheep, and cattle in the German town of Hanau. Hanau was in the Kingdom of Hesse-Cassel, which was one of the many kingdoms that divided Germany two hundred years ago (the largest German kingdom was Prussia). The brothers' father was the town clerk of Hanau. He liked nothing better than to wear a uniform and to have his children respond to him in military fashion. Their mother was kindly and hard-working. She always seemed to be sewing new clothes for the children or knitting sweaters for them. The whole family was very close, affectionate, and loyal. They lived during a time of great changes in Europe. It was a time of strife and revolutions and the Napoleonic Wars. In spite of this, or perhaps because of it, the Grimm family was always very interested in their German heritage.

10

In 1796, when Jacob was eleven and Wilhelm was ten, their father died. Two years later, the brothers moved to the town of Cassel for further schooling; their childhood days were over. When their studies were completed, they decided to study law. They enrolled at Marburg University where Jacob became friends with one of the young instructors, Freidrich Karl von Savigny. Savigny collected books and manuscripts of medieval literature (from about 700 A.D. to 1500). Jacob was in awe of the collection. He spent a great deal of time at the professor's house studying the ancient material. As a result, Savigny invited Jacob to go with him to Paris for a year to research the history of Roman law in the Middle Ages. Jacob gladly accepted the opportunity. But it was the first time that the brothers had been separated. They missed each other terribly. When they were reunited at last, they both swore they would never part again.

13

On October 14, 1806, Napoleon conquered Prussia and all of Germany fell to the French. Napoleon established new order and new thrones. He appointed his brother Jérôme Bonaparte to be king of the new kingdom of Westphalia, which included parts of the kingdom where the Brothers Grimm lived. The royal headquarters was in Cassel. Two years later, in 1808, Jacob and Wilhelm's mother died. Jacob, now twenty-three years old, became head of the family, a position he held for the rest of his life. By now the brothers had finished school. But they did not choose legal careers. They wanted work that would give them time to research old German literature. Luckily, both of them were hired as librarians for the royal library. Their free hours were spent collecting German folksongs and tales, which would later make them famous. Then, through Jacob's friend Savigny, they met Clemens Brentano and Achim von Arnim who also loved the German past and collected ancient literature. Brentano and Arnim invited the brothers to contribute a few of their folksongs to a book called *Wunderhorn* that Arnim was about to publish. By bartering as they had in childhood, Jacob and Wilhelm traded their songs for stories to add to their collection of old tales.

The brothers worked together side by side at the same desk and arranged their books for each other's convenience. They continued to collect old tales from family members and friends. Many of the tales, such as *Snow White, Little Red Riding Hood,* and *Sleeping Beauty*, came from Marie Müller; she was the nanny for the Wild family, who owned the only drugstore in Cassel. Some of Marie's tales were French stories that had changed over the years as they were told in German to each new generation of children. In the version told 200 years earlier in France, Little Red Riding Hood was swallowed by the wolf and that was the end of the story. As told by Marie, Red Riding Hood was saved by a woodsman in a happy ending. Marie kept the brothers busy writing down her tales. However, gathering other stories was not so easy. One woman had told some stories to the Grimms' friend Brentano, but he had not written them down. When Jacob and Wilhelm went to see her, she would not tell her stories again because she thought people would laugh at her. Even the brothers' eagerness to barter for the tales could not change her mind.

The brothers wandered around the countryside searching for more tales. Under Jacob's careful eye, Wilhelm rewrote the tales, often adding new details. In *Sleeping Beauty*, Marie simply said that everyone fell asleep in the castle, "even the flies on the wall." The remark about the flies gave Wilhelm an idea for expanding the tale. He added what was happening elsewhere in the castle at the precise moment everyone fell asleep. He included horses in the stable, dogs in the courtyard, pigeons on the roof, even the cook who was about to cuff the kitchen boy for a misdeed. The brothers constantly sought to improve the tales and were not yet ready to publish them. Then one day Arnim came to read them. He paraded around the room, dropping page after page on the floor while a pet canary perched comfortably on his head. Arnim insisted that the Grimm brothers publish the collection.

19

In December 1812, the year Napoleon's army met with defeat in Russia, the first volume of *Grimms' Fairy Tales* was published. In writing down the stories, Jacob and Wilhelm had hoped to keep the German heritage alive; they wanted to make their work available for scholars to study. They hadn't given much thought to the children who would enjoy the tales, so they were surprised when families eagerly bought their book to read at home. The brothers quickly set to work on a second collection of tales. This book was much easier to do than the first, because stories came to them from all over. The Grimms didn't have to leave the house. People came pounding on their door with stories. Some knew about the brothers' bartering ways and wanted to trade. The boldest was an old soldier who exchanged his stories for the brothers' old trousers.

Grimms' Fairy Tales became popular partly because they helped to restore German national pride. But they also matched the mood of the time. In the Romantic period, people believed that creative powers worked best when the imagination was allowed to flow freely. To escape from the problems of the present, artists and writers turned to faraway places, the medieval past, and the folklore and legends of the common people. Such a movement was appropriate for the troubled times of the Brothers Grimm. So their next volume of tales was eagerly awaited. For the new collection Jacob and Wilhelm had a lucky encounter. They met a genuine storyteller, Frau Katharina Dorothea Viehmann. She lived in a village near Cassel and delivered eggs and butter to friends of the Grimms. Happily for the brothers, she was not a difficult barterer. She settled for rolls and coffee in exchange for her stories.

22

Frau Viehmann told the Grimm brothers more than twenty tales. She had an unequaled gift for retaining the stories firmly in her mind, pure and unspoiled. It was fortunate chance that Jacob and Wilhelm saved her treasure trove of stories, for she died in 1815, only a year after the second volume of fairy tales was published. Her most famous story, *Cinderella*, had evolved from a French tale called *The Little Fur Slipper*. Since the French word for fur, "vair," is similar to the French word for glass, which is "verre," the fur slipper became glass in the second volume of *Grimms' Fairy Tales*. Thanks to Frau Viehmann, the glass slipper went on to make fortunes for the manufacturers of glass slipper novelties for the next hundred and fifty years.

25

The success of the fairy tales brought world-wide fame to the Grimm brothers. They had many visitors: professors, scholars, writers, and the merely curious. The visitors all wanted to meet the famous brothers. One day Hans Christian Andersen came to call. Jacob sent him away. He did not know that Hans Christian Andersen was the famous Danish author of many original tales for children, including *Thumbelina* and *The Little Mermaid*. Wilhelm was not home at the time. When he found out, he was horrified that such an important visitor had been turned away. But Jacob had been busy working on a German grammar book that was to establish his reputation as a philologist—a person who studies literature and its relation to human speech. While he was at work on his grammar book, he had left the collecting of fairy tales to Wilhelm. He had gotten out of touch with people involved in the world of make-believe.

27

On May 15, 1825, thirty-nine-year-old Wilhelm married Dorothea Wild, the druggist's daughter. She was seven years younger than Wilhelm and had been his friend for a long time. The marriage did not change things between Jacob and Wilhelm. Jacob continued to live in the same house with Dorothea and Wilhelm and was a loving uncle to their three children. Wilhelm rose first in the morning to read his Greek testament. At mid-morning he joined Dorothea and Jacob for coffee and then the two brothers went to work—side-by-side—the same as ever. In the afternoon they went for walks together. In the evening they would rejoin the family for supper. This close relationship is revealed by their signing many of their books *Brothers Grimm*. Their name has become a symbol of brotherly friendship and creative cooperation.

29

Second in importance to the *Fairy Tales* was the Grimms' publication of *German Folk Tales*. Folk tales differ from fairy tales because their roots are in reality, a specific place or event in history. Fairy tales are timeless and pure fantasy, often taking place in a medieval setting. Grimms' *Folk Tales* include *The Pied Piper of Hamlin*. This tale is believed to be based on an actual event in history—the Children's Crusade of 1212, when armies of children from Germany and France marched to the Holy Land and were never seen again. By publishing these treasures of German heritage, the brothers brought much honor to their country. However, one person did not think so—Prince William II, ruler of Hesse-Cassel. The German royal family had reclaimed the throne of their kingdom just before Napoleon was defeated at Waterloo in 1815. William II refused to give the brothers the higher salary they requested. Insulted, they accepted an offer from Göttingen University in the Kingdom of Hanover. "So the Grimms are leaving," said William II sarcastically. "What a loss! They have never done anything for me."

31

More misfortune fell upon the Grimms after their move. The Duke of Cumberland had become King of Hanover. He was English and was related to Queen Victoria. He wrote a new constitution for the country. The Grimm brothers and five other scholars and teachers swore loyalty to the old constitution, which the new king wanted to replace. So he had them banished from the kingdom. The Grimms went back to Cassel, where they earned no money for two years. However, they set to work on the first complete dictionary of the German language. It was to serve as the model for dictionaries in other languages. To do the work, the brothers had to refer to huge numbers of books which were stacked on tables and against walls in several rooms. Looking things up meant a lot of work! Fortunately, it did not keep the brothers from forging ahead with their challenging project.

The news of the Grimms' new dictionary reached the King of Prussia. He invited the brothers to come and live in Berlin to work on their dictionary with "the use of all aid and support available." The brothers responded, "We strive for nothing but the opportunity to devote our remaining days to the achievement of the work which relates to the language and history of our beloved fatherland." They moved at once to Berlin. Friends and scholars eagerly awaited their arrival. They moved into a house with ten rooms near a school for Wilhelm's three children, Herman, Rudolf, and Auguste. Soon the house became too small for the active children and the parties they held. The family moved again, but were in the new house only a short time, because Wilhelm forgot to pay the rent while away at a conference. Their final move was to a house next to the railroad station. Suddenly, the brothers, who were used to quiet and solitude and walks in the countryside, liked the hustle and bustle of the big city. They looked forward to living there happily ever after.

35

﹏ EPILOGUE ﹏

When Jacob died on September 20, 1863, he was buried in Berlin next to his brother Wilhelm who had died four years earlier on December 16, 1859. Like the characters in one of their tales, they had become folk heroes. Their complete writings filled sixty-two volumes. In addition they contributed four books to the thirty-two volume German dictionary that was not completed until 1962. Even so, most people think of them as "The Fairytale Brothers." This is because their best-loved work is *Grimms' Fairy Tales*, which has become a household book in many lands and in seventy languages. In Russia alone over 18,000,000 copies have been sold. About the collection, Wilhelm said, "In the fairy tales a world of magic is opened up before us, one which still exists among us in a secret forest, in underground caves, and in the deepest sea, and is still available to children." But without the Brothers Grimm, the "world of magic" that they preserved would have been lost to us forever.